Looking Back

DOUGLAS COUNTY, NEVADA

Published by Pediment Publishing, a division of The Pediment Group, Inc. www.pediment.com

The Settelmeyer family, 2007, proud sponsors of this project. *Photo by Shannon Litz/The Record-Courier*

Foreword

Douglas County is blessed with a rich history built on a strong foundation of agriculture and its companion industries. The cornerstones, laid in place by our pioneer families and expanded by their descendants, have provided decades of an extensive visual record seen here in the pages of "Looking Back."

This coffee table hard bound pictorial history book offers a snapshot of our Valley's history, a glimpse in time, an insight into the people that helped this Valley grow. It is a reflection of close-knit communities, families and friends, working closely together through the generations to give Douglas County the fascinating heritage we enjoy here today.

I hope you find this commemorative book enjoyable and informative about the people, friends and generations of families who have lived, and still live, in Douglas County.

The Record-Courier is pleased to have the opportunity to publish "Looking Back." The photos are courtesy of Douglas County Historical Society, The Carson Valley Museum & Cultural Center, The Genoa Court House Museum, The Record-Courier and the private collections from the many gracious people of Douglas County.

This historical illustration of time and evaluation could not have been possible without recognizing those who devoted their time and efforts to make it happen. Many thanks to Kurt Hildebrand, editor of The Record-Courier; The Record-Courier staff members Jonni Hill and Scott Neuffer; Town of Genoa Historian, Billie Jean Rightmire; Grace Bower, Marlena Hellwinkel providing historical reseach and verification of historical fact, Lynette Cameron, Marketing Director for Sierra Nevada Media Group and the people of Douglas County.

Keith Tanoos
Publisher, The Record-Courier

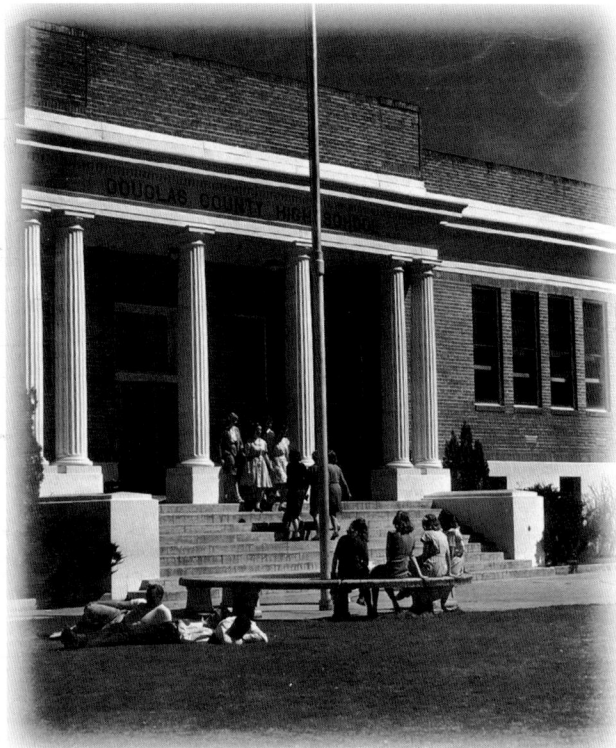

Table of Contents

The Late 1800s

The late 1800s saw a move of Douglas County's center from its founding in Genoa to the central Valley with the foundation and development of the town of Gardnerville.

Gardnerville was founded in 1879 by Lawrence Gilman and named after property owner John Gardner. Gilman moved the Kent House from Genoa to Gardnerville and renamed it after the new town. It took a few years for the new town to take off. In 1885, Gilman sold half of his interest in the town, which consisted of a post office, hotel, lodging house, blacksmith and wagon shot and a saloon, for $1,250.

By the 1890s, Gardnerville was firmly established as a town and some of its current structures came into being. Charles Brown built the East Fork Hotel in 1893. The two-story building that is now the J.T. Basque Bar & Dining Room was moved from Virginia City in 1896. William Ritchford built the hotel that bears his name in 1898. All three buildings still stand in downtown Gardnerville today.

According to the Genoa Courier in August 1896, Gardnerville consisted of three hotels, three stores, four saloons, two blacksmith shops and three barbershops.

Left: The A.C. Pratt house in Genoa, built in 1874. A.C. Pratt and George Smith at gate. Pratt's son, Zenas on porch. The white building at the rear is the printing office of the Courier, Pratt's Douglas County Newspaper. *(DCHS 131.G.358)*

Right: Steam engine tractor, owned by Dangberg Company, used to haul firewood. Each wagon carried five cords of wood. *(DCHS 334-G-020)*

Above: Leander Hawkins, first surveyor of Genoa. His map became the "Trustee Map" of 1874. *(DCHS 0010.G.010)*

Right: Glenbrook, Lake Tahoe, 1876. View of Glenbrook Bay showing sawmills, breakwater, and steamers Carson and Tahoe Lumber and Flume Co. and also lake terminus of Lake Tahoe Narrow Gauge Railroad. *(DCHS 0005-G-116)*

Top right: Raycraft family, 1905. From left are Jack, Josephine (Hellwinkel), Annie, Ellen (grandma), Tom and Richard. *(DCHS 0131-G-323)*

Opposite: Gardnerville Hotel, circa 1875. *(DCHS 0137.H-59)*

Above: Legendary stage driver Hank Monk at the reins of Doc Benton's stage, circa 1880. These stages made periodic trips from Carson Valley to Lake Tahoe.

Courtesy Lake Tahoe Historical Society

Left: Frank Craven's team and others at Spooner Station, 1880s. Craven's team of 24 head of horses and mule's hauled V & T Engine to Lake Tahoe over Kingsbury Summit in August 1875. *(DCHS 2003.48.27)*

Above: Gardnerville Hotel, circa 1880. *(DCHS 0056.G.0001e)*

Right: Private school in Genoa at the Kinsey house in the 1880s. *(DCHS 10.G.8)*

Above: Wood drive on the Carson River, 1880-1890. *(DCHS 131-L-583)*

Left: Portrait of Marrie L. Morris, October 29, 1886. Morris married Frank Golden of the Golden Hotel. *(DCHS 0131.G.369)*

Far left: Glenbrook loggers, late 1800s. *(DCHS 0388-G-0001)*

Below: A. C. Pratt published the Carson Valley News in the 1870s. *(DCHS 0131.G.364)*

Right: Genoa students & teachers, 1889. *(DCHS 137.H.320)*

Far right: Cohn family at a picnic, June 28, 1891.
(DCHS 0137.H.749r)

Below: Miller Residence in Millerville, circa 1888. House was moved from Virginia City to this location and was moved again to Dayton where it stands today. *(DCHS 137.H.215)*

Left: Elizabeth Wilson Miller, 1890.
(DCHS 0137.H.0076)

Above: Wedding portrait of Mr. and Mrs. Henry Frevert. *(DCHS 0014.G.003)*

Right: Wood products are loaded on the train at Spooners Summit, 1876.
(DCHS 334-G-022)

Right: Arnold and Charlotte Settelmeyer wedding photo, December 17, 1890. *(DCHS 137-H-6986)*

Middle: Mr. and Mrs. Fritz Dressler, 1890. *(DCHS 0131.G.312)*

Above: Wedding portrait of Walter and Anna Frey, August 16, 1893. Walter was born near Genoa in 1870 and Anna arrived in Genoa in 1885. *(DCHS 0150.G.002)*

Left: Lakeshore House, 1893, currently J.T.'s. *(DCHS 334-G-1w)*

15

Above: George Washington Gale Ferris, inventor of the Great Ferris Wheel on Midway Plaisance, circa 1893. *(DCHS 0005.G.061a)*

Right: P.C. Wilder & Co. General Merchandise, first store in Gardnerville, 1895. *(DCHS 0088.G.008)*

Above: Douglas County Bicycle Club, circa 1895. Photo includes, Henry Helberg, William Hussman, Otto Hussman, Maurice Mack, Joseph Cardinal, and Henry Mack. *(DCHS 296.G.25)*

Left: Gov. Erin Boyle and Captain Pete Mayo, chief of the Nevada Washo, circa 1865. *(DCHS 0131.L.569)*

Far left: Mrs. M. A. Ferris, wife of George W. Ferris on December 11, 1895. *(DCHS 0005.G.060a)*

Above: A freight company with long teams of horses pulling freight, late 1800s. *(DCHS 2007-003-0)*

Right: Alexander Miller Residence in Millerville, circa 1895. *(DCHS 137.H.217)*

Left: Centerville Bar, Carson Valley, 1896. *(DCHS 2005-004-002)*

Below: Grinding barley on F. W. Stodieck Ranch in 1896. The horse-operated equipment is a power sweep. *(DCHS 0131-H-625a)*

Above: Rahbeck Hotel, featuring "Hot and Cold Baths," Gardnerville, 1899. *(DCHS 1095.G.017)*

Left: Frederick Hugh Dressler at nine months old in May, 1899. *(DCHS 0210.G.010k)*

Opposite: Gardnerville Cornet Band, the towns first band, circa 1897. Back row are E. Jarvis, F. Luhrs, Wm. Rabe, Wm. King, Geo Brown, M. Christensen, L.P. Jacobsen and Wm. Nelson. Middle row are H. Berning, L.M. Jacobsen, Carl Henningsen, Clarence Henningsen, F. Frantzen, W. Luhrs and H. Luhrs. Front row are Earl Christensen, F. Berning, Bert Selkirk, Henry Elges and Fritz Elges. *(DCHS 1045.G.1a)*

The Early 1900s

The first two decades of the 1900s were a time of growth that would change the face of the Carson Valley forever. The Virginia and Truckee Railway cut a swath of steam and steel through the Carson Valley on its first run, June 12, 1906, along a right of way granted by the H. F. Dangberg Land and Livestock Company. The line terminated at the newly established town of Minden in 1906.

A decade later, Minden-Gardnerville had become the center of commerce and population in the Carson Valley. Sentiment grew to move the county seat, then located in Genoa, to the Minden-Gardnerville area. On April 5, 1915, a resolution was adopted by the Board of County Commissioners, accepting a deed from the H. F. Dangberg Land and Livestock Company conveying the property in the town of Minden to Douglas County for a new courthouse and county jail, at the same time granting the high school location to Gardnerville.

On January 1,1916, Minden was officially designated the county seat of Douglas County and the hub of ranching and mining concerns in the Carson Valley and surrounding areas.

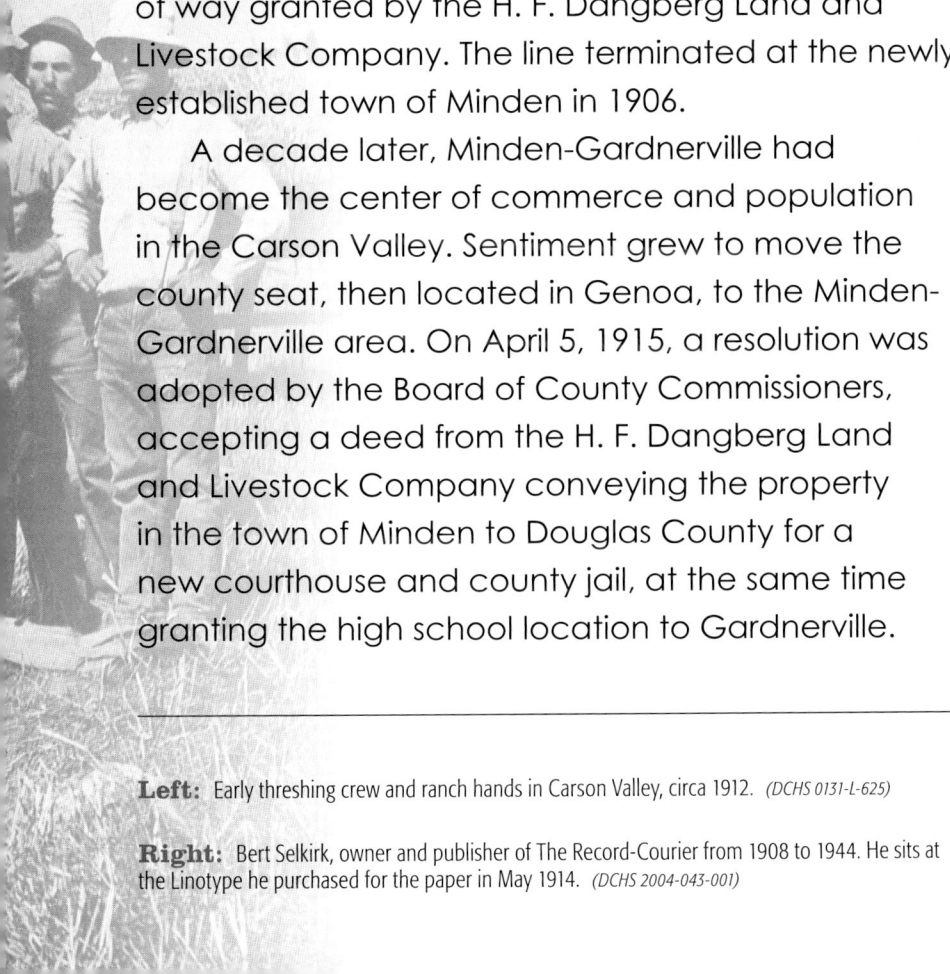

Left: Early threshing crew and ranch hands in Carson Valley, circa 1912. *(DCHS 0131-L-625)*

Right: Bert Selkirk, owner and publisher of The Record-Courier from 1908 to 1944. He sits at the Linotype he purchased for the paper in May 1914. *(DCHS 2004-043-001)*

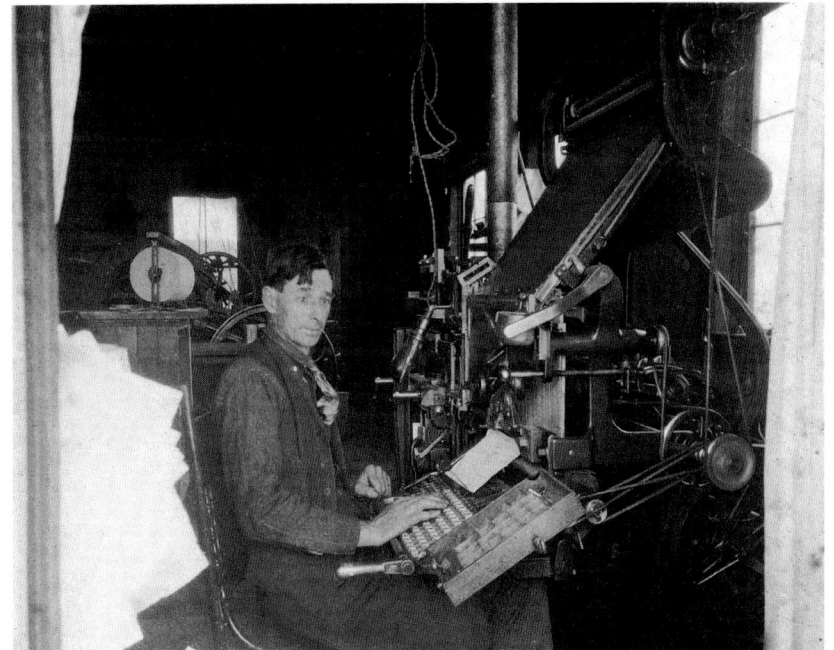

Right: Julia Stewart, circa 1900. *(DCHS 2006.089.035)*

Above: View of the I.O.O.F. building, church and courthouse in Genoa, circa 1900.
(DCHS 0137.H.668)

Left: Wovoka (Jake Wilson), left, Paiute and creator of the Ghost Dance, and cowboy, Tim McCoy in early 1900s.
(DCHS 2006.058.348)

Far left: Overland Hotel, Gardnerville, early 1900s.
(DCHS 0195.G.020)

Above: Gardnerville Methodist Church, 1900. *(DCHS 0137.H.058)*

Below: Douglas County football team in the early 1900s. *(DCHS 0165.G.001)*

Above: Lodge members from Gardnerville, posed on the capital steps in Carson City, circa 1900. *(DCHS 0260.G.0098H)*

Top: Trinity Lutheran Church. Back row are Maggie Stodieck, John Henry Stodieck with Douglas, Bill Hussman, Grandpa Bassman, Bill Elges, Ludwig Ruhenstroth, Louis Stodieck, Dietrick Tholke, Dick Bassman, Friedrich W. Stodieck, Fritz Schacht, and John Crawley. Middle row are Barbara Glock, Minnie Hussman, Grandma Bassman, Minister Horsman, Ida Ruhenstroth with baby Henry, Mrs. Helena Stodieck, Mrs. Dick Bassman with Earnhardt, Mrs. Adele Stodieck with Cecil, Mrs. Schacht with Arthur, and Mrs. Horsman with her baby. Front row are Alvina Hussman (Kidman), unknown, Luwine Ruhenstroth, unknown, Fred Berning, unknown, unknown, Erna Berning, Harold Hussman, August Schacht, and Mabel Schacht. *(DCHS 0137.H.214)*

Above: Herman Scheele with his team and milk wagon, circa 1900. Scheele would transport milk daily from the Fredricksburg area to the Douglas County Creamery at Waterloo as a means to support his family. *(DCHS 0309-G-1)*

Above: Douglas County Creamery Co., 1911. The long ramp with team and wagon on it was designed to utilize gravity in operating the creamery. *(DCHS 137.H.326)*

Right: First locally owned threshing machine owned by Brockliss Brothers, early 1900s. *(DCHS 0131-G-379)*

Above: Bailing hay in Carson Valley, early 1900s. *(DCHS 0225-G-008)*

Left: Early wood cutting machine in Douglas County. *(DCHS 0137-H-123)*

Top: Golden Crown mill. *(DCHS 0131-G-463e)*

Left: Early equipment.
(DCHS 0281-G-21L)

Right: Portrait of William J. Hawkins, circa 1900. Son of Mr. and Mrs. John Hawkins, William was the first white boy born in Washoe City. *(DCHS 0131.G.414)*

Above: The William F. Bull family, circa 1900. From the back left, Annie, Mary Jones (John's twin), Janet Park, Robert, Agnes, Elizabeth "Lizzie" Stock. Front row, Mrs. Agnes Bull (William's wife), Fred, John (Mary's twin), Victor, George, and Mr. William F. Bull. The man with the white beard is Mr. William Fields, a friend of the family. *(DCHS 0179.G.0500)*

Left: Hans Jepsen in the wagon in front of the community post office and store, circa 1900. *(DCHS 0260.G.0982)*

POST OFFICE

STORE

Left: Henry and Edna Tillman in their Genoa home, circa 1900. They are enjoying a family musical with father and mother Tillman and brother John looking down on them. *(DCHS 137-01-94)*

Middle: Jim and Joe Raycraft take a trip into Carson City for a formal portrait, circa 1900. The stage driver, Barney McCaffery, gets in the picture as well, right. *(DCHS 0131.G.001a)*

Above: Wedding portrait of William Champagne and Edna Tillman, circa 1900. *(DCHS 0216.G.091)*

Right: Gelatt Livery Stable, Genoa. Destroyed by 1910 fire. *(DCHS 0137-H-106)*

Above: A twelve-mule team shipping hay, circa 1900. *(DCHS 137.H.124)*

Left: Gray's blacksmith shop, early 1900s. The shop was at the northwest corner of the rebuilt stockade. Identified are William Daniel Gray in center with his sons William Joseph (in light hat) and Morton Thomas Gray in dark hat. Frank Walker is in the buggy. *(DCHS 0137-H-109)*

Below: Glenbrook Pier, early 1900s. *(DCHS 0281-G-21k)*

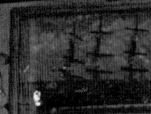

Above: The Theo Tillman Home in Genoa, circa, 1900. From left, Henry Tillman, Edna Tillman, and Theo Tillman. *(DCHS 216.G.98)*

Left: Corner Saloon, Gardnerville. *(DCHS 0082-0008)*

Far left: Oberon Saloon, owner Pop Starke, Gardnerville, 1906. *(DCHS 131-G-443)*

Top: Gardnerville Grammar School, circa 1900. *(DCHS 137.H.61)*

Right: Mill at Glenbrook. Glenbrook was the most important early settlement in the Tahoe area. It was the economic, industrial, transportation, and social hub.
Courtesy Douglas County Historical Society

Above: Stephen A. Kinsey Residence before remodeling in Genoa. *(DCHS 137.H.213)*

Left: Jim Brockliss threshing crew, circa 1900. Crew members, from left, top row are William Park who later became Douglas County sheriff; James J. Brockliss, owner of the Sheridan Blacksmith Shop; unknown; Arthur E. Brockliss who later became the owner of the Sheridan Hotel and Bar and was also Postmaster of the town; William A. Brockliss at Arthur's right, learned the carpentry trade and built many of the early day homes in the Carson Valley; Arthur (Tex) Park, brother of William Park; Bill Kemp, local carpenter and farm hand and a former Mother Lode miner; Anthony (Tony) Brockliss Jr. was the eldest son of the 13 Brockliss children. Bottom row are Francis E. (Frank) Brockliss, studied law in the offices of D.W. Virgin, then District Attorney of Douglas County. Frank was later elected to the Nevada State Legislature then he went on to serve as the District Attorney of Douglas County for 16 years. The man standing next to Frank is unidentified, and the Washoe Indians. *(DCHS 0249-G-0002b)*

Above: Oldest house in the state of Nevada built in Genoa in 1851 and was destroyed by fire June 28, 1910, circa 1905. *(DCHS 0075.G.0001)*

Right: Interior of Dempster's Ice Cream Parlor in Gardnerville, early 1900s. *(DCHS 0089.G.16)*

Above: An early hay press in Carson Valley. Sitting in the box is Wm. Hansen. The forker on hay stack is Arthur Brockliss. Standing in front of wheel on water wagon is Tony Brockliss. By fly wheel on engine is William Morrison. Standing on separator is Jim Brockliss. *(DCHS 0131-G-454)*

Right: Glenbrook loggers taking a break from loading logs on the train at the pier. *Courtesy Douglas County Historical Society*

Above: Carson Valley Mercantile was owned by Earl Christensen and Chris H. Neddenriep. *(DCHS 0193.6.001)*

Below: Land clearing and ditch digging crew ready to leave for several weeks to bring sagebrush under cultivation, early 1900s. Notice the cook house and feed rack on wagon. *(DCHS 0005-G-103)*

Left: Pete Heitman Ranch, 1905. *(DCHS 137-G-604)*

Right: Dr. Eliza Cook, right, circa 1905. *(DCHS 0131.G.322)*

Above: A horse-drawn sleigh in front of The Sheridan General Merchandise store of Barrett and Tucke, early 1900s. The second floor was a dance hall. *(DCHS 0137-H-108)*

Right: H. C. Jepsen family and residence in Genoa, circa 1905. *(DCHS 0139.G.008)*

Right: Central School class of 1906.
(DCHS 225.G.16)

Above: View of Walley's Hot Springs, circa 1905. *(DCHS 0136-H-159)*

Left: Horse-drawn buggy in front of Sheridan Hotel, 1906. *(DCHS 0083.6.001a)*

Left: Douglas County Creamery Co., September 10, 1908. *(DCHS 137.4.139)*

Below: Farming crew, circa 1906. The gentleman second from right with hand on hips, is Henry Godecke. Seated on the ground to his right are three of his sons, from right, Henry Herman, Edward F.H., and Clarence William. *(DCHS 0375-H-0782A)*

Above: The Douglas County officials of 1908 in front of the courthouse doors in Genoa. Back row, from left, Fred Klotz, auditor and recorder, Ely Wyatt, sheriff, Judge Daniel Webster Virgin. Front, from left, Leo Springmeyer, John Thompsen and James Campbell, county commissioners, and Hans C. Jepsen, county clerk and treasurer. *(DCHS 0088.G.015.15a)*

Right: Martha Graunke's Candy Store and Ice Cream Parlor, Gardnerville, 1908. *(DCHS 0281.G.21d)*

Below: The Douglas County Commissioners and other officials in session in 1908. Included in the photo, Fred Klotz, Hans C. Jepsen, Frank Brockliss, Ely Wyatt, Fritz Schacht, "Pop" Starke, and J. C. Thompsen. *(DCHS 0088.G.014)*

Above: Farmer's Bank of Carson Valley in Minden with Mr. Marsh (bank cashier) and Doris Dangberg standing in front. When the new building was erected across the street, this building became the U.S. Post Office. *(DCHS 0005.G.078)*

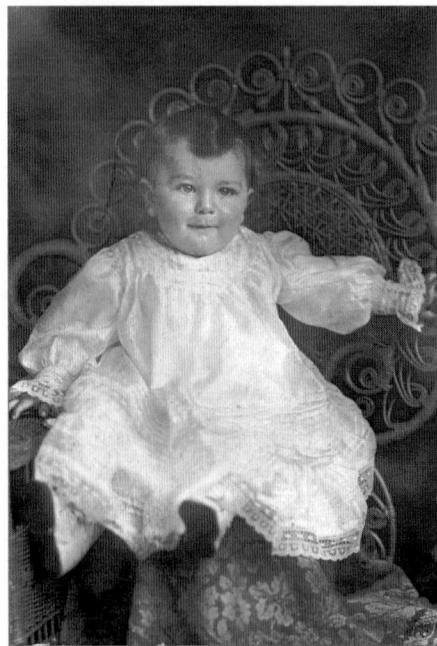

Left: Arthur Champagne, son of William and Edna in 1909. *(DCHS 0216.G.092)*

Far left: Gardnerville Public School, circa 1908. *(DCHS 137.H.63)*

Above: Trinity Lutheran Church confirmation class, 1909. Back row are Richard Fricke, George Settelmeyer, Henry Godecke, Edward Godecke, Katherine Settelmeyer (shorter girl), Clara Kruse, Pastor Menzel, Dora Heidtman, Bill Lampe, Arendt Jensen, Anna Heise, Bertha Cordes Lundergreen. Front row are Wm. F. Neddenriep, Pauline Jepsen, Fritz Syll, Dorathea Heise (wearing glasses), Sadie Neddenriep Lampe (wearing necklace), Tillie Neddenriep Rich and Hans Jensen. *(DCHS 2005.006.015)*

Right: Lutheran Church picnic in Gardnerville, June 23, 1909. *(DCHS 119-L-7)*

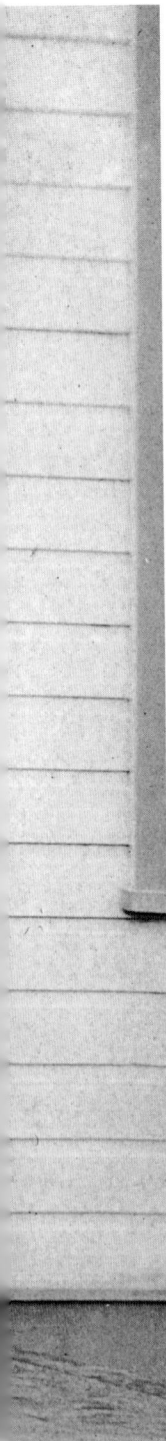

Above: Douglas County Creamery Co., September 10, 1908. *(DCHS 0281.G.021c)*

Left: Washoe, Clara Frank and her baby in early 1900s. *(DCHS 137-H-242a)*

Far left: Gardnerville School third and fourth graders with Teacher Kate O'Hara in 1909. Back row, Elvin Stodieck, Gustava Lundergreen, Harry Winkelman, Smithie McMullin, and Sigsbe Lundergreen. Middle row, Agnes Jensen, Florence Heitman, Effie Imelli, Norma Dangberg, Vincent Neilson, Henry Frevert, Norman Brown, Ernest Hogrefe, Andrew Jespersen, and Willie Chistensen. Front row, Edna Hellwinkel, Lottie Syll, Raymond Jones, Clara Imelli, and Lizzie Syll. *(DCHS 2005.006.017)*

Below: Student class picture from the Stewart Indian School. Photo, circa 1910. *(DCHS 2006.058.122)*

Above: Crystal Bazaar and Minden Inn, circa 1910. *(DCHS 0120.G.175)*

Right: Meyers Mercantile Company in Minden. The building was dedicated in 1907, circa 1915. *(DCHS 0137.H.153)*

Left: Farmer's Bank in Minden, circa 1910.
(DCHS 0120.G.177)

Above: Gardnerville Trinity Lutheran Church, early 1900s.
(DCHS 0225.G.006)

Right: Douglas flour mill, Gardnerville. *(DCHS no number
(Same as 0066-0001 and 0066-0005))*

Above: Wool loaded for market on a trailer hauled by a team of 12 horses. *(DCHS 0137-H-0620)*

Right: Local men gather to enjoy their favorite brew, circa 1910. *(DCHS 0119.L.005)*

Below: Ricky cowboys on horseback at Topaz. Matt Koenig on buckskin horse on the end and Joe Koenig on gray horse on the right in front of the Old Topaz Post Office headquarters. *(DCHS 0049-H-778)*

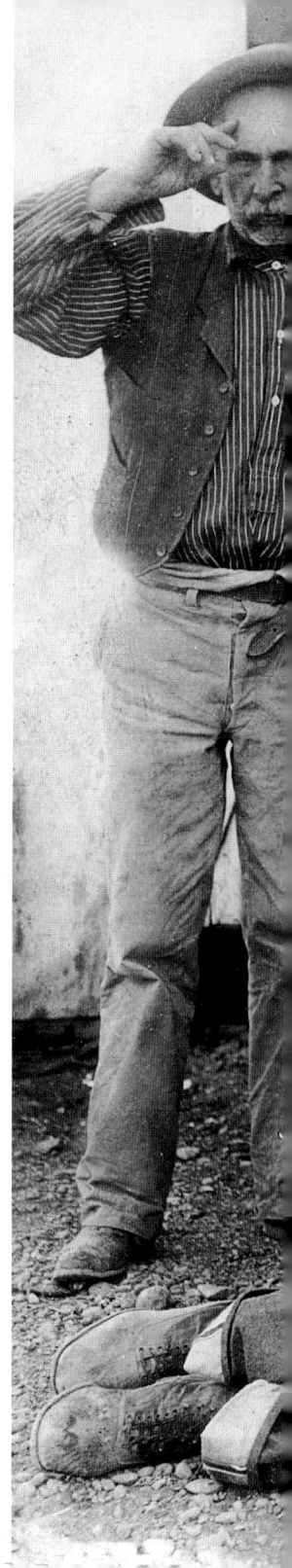

Above: Minden Butter Manufacturing Co., early 1900s. *(DCHS 0137-H-064)*

Above: Minden school house, circa 1910. *(DCHS 0005.G.204)*

Left: A Gardnerville auto parade on July 4th, 1911. *(DCHS 0153.6.002)*

Right: Douglas County High School with principal E. O. Vaughn, back left, 1912. Photo includes, Polly Pepsen, Arlie Jones, Lola Jepsen, Anna Heise, Juanita Frey, Grace Jones, Hazel Fowler, Grace Daughey, Lenora Jessen, Irma Settelmeyer, Minnie Springmeyer, Si Krummes, John Brown, Hans Jensen, Pat Harris, Louis Nelson, Halvo Jacobsen, Bill Lampe, Carl Springmeyer, Fred Hellwinkel, Herman Springmeyer, George Henningsen, Ed Godecke, Walter Williams, George Settelmeyer, Fred Beck, Henry Godecke, L. Lange, Arendt Jensen, Fred Settelmeyer, Carol Haugner. *(DCHS 0005.G.37)*

Left: Grace Dangberg, circa 1912. *(DCHS 0137.H.282)*

Far left: Frieda Heise and William Wennhold wedding at the Heise Ranch, 1912. *(DCHS 289-G-1)*

51

Left: Five wagon loads of grain delivered to Minden Flour Mill from Dangberg and Buckeye Ranch, circa 1913. *(DCHS 0005-G-109)*

Far left: Harry Hawkins, Gardnerville physician who built the Carson Valley Hospital in 1914. *(DCHS 0281.G.062)*

Below: Townspeople in front of Genoa Court House, circa 1913. From left, Hans R. Jepsen, Attorney George A. Montrose, Judge Frank P. Langan, Court Reporter Felice Cohen, County Clerk Hans C. Jepsen, Andy Arrild, Sheriff Al Jarvis, Joe Cardinal, William Dangberg, Ezra Jarvis, Judge Daniel Webster Virgin, Frank Jones, District Attorney Frank Brockliss, and T.P. Hawkins. *Courtesy Douglas County Historical Society*

53

Above: Gilman Hotel, Genoa, early 1900s. *(DCHS 88.G.006)*

Right: Trinity Lutheran Church confirmation class, March 16, 1913. Back row are, Florence Heitman, Erna Schacht, Pastor Menzel, Edward Berning, Gustava (Lundergreen) Howard and Rosie Cordes. Front row are George May (Marquat) Settelmeyer, Ada (Marquat) Storke, Alma (Settelmeyer) Fricke and Hans Jensen. *(DCHS 2005.006.019)*

Top: Douglas Flour Mill, Upper Carson Valley. *(DCHS no number (same as 0020-0025))*

Left: Tahoe steamer, circa 1915. *(DCHS 2006-058-058)*

Above: Early 1900s portrait of Jennie Jacobsen, daughter of Peter and Caroline Jacobsen. *(DCHS 0281.G.21g)*

Right: Cutting and threshing grain with a combined harvester powered with a Best steamer, circa 1915. *(DCHS 0005-G-158)*

Above: Engine No. 22. *(DCHS 2006-058-363)*

Below: Highway scene in Gardnerville, circa 1915. *(DCHS Black album in vault)*

Above: Douglas County High School students who attended classes in Gardnerville school in 1915 included, from left bottom row, Alma Settelmeyer Fricke, Alyse Springmeyer Faletti, Grace Wilder, Lillian Jacobsen Logan, Jennie Jacobsen, Ada Fricke, Hilda Heise Burr, Anna Neddenriep Dressler, and Viola Harris; second row, Florence Heitman, Sadie Belle Brown, Aletha Nielsen, Agnes Jensen, Vera Wilder, Alma Anderson Jacobsen, Ruth Atcheson, Gladys Dangberg Brinkman, Irma Settelmeyer, and Effie Imelli Miller; third row, Siegfried Heise, James Peterson, Ed Lampe, Hans Jepsen, Halvor Jacobsen, Fred Dressler, Walter Haugner, Willie Christiansen, and principal Theodore S. Hook. *(DCHS 0190.G.7)*

Left: Minden School, circa 1915. *(DCHS 0005-G-0079)*

Right: Wedding portrait of Raymond and Gorgonia Borda on December 15th, 1917.

(DCHS 2003.55.001)

Far right: Minden Inn, circa 1915. *(DCHS Black album in vault)*

Above: Trinity Lutheran Church confirmation class of June 1, 1919. Standing are Albert Bowman, Douglas Stodieck, Rev. Menzel and Cecil Stodieck. Seated are Walter Wennhold, Gertrude Luhrs, Arthur Cordes, Sofena Lampe and Earnhart Bassman. *(DCHS 0226.G.020)*

Left: Main Street, Gardnerville, circa 1915. *(DCHS Black album in vault)*

Above: Gardnerville Grammar School, circa 1916. *(DCHS 88.G.4)*

Right: School in Genoa, 1919. *(DCHS 90.G.11)*

Above: Post Office Gardnerville, IOOF Hall, Howard Brothers General Merchandise, Gasolene, circa 1917. *(DCHS 0137.H.54)*

Left: H. C. Jepsen, county clerk and treasurer in his office at the courthouse. *(DCHS 0260.G.0981)*

The 1920s

The 20s saw the era of the automobile and mechanization. Improved roads began to crisscross the Valley to accommodate the modern transportation. Prohibition tied the hands of many business owners and created a whole new illicit industry in the Valley for some enterprising Valley folks. It was April of 1924 when prohibition enforcement officers oozed into town and, before their identity was revealed, staged a raid on the Overland Hotel, securing a quantity of liquor and the arrest of the proprietor, John Etchemendy, bartender William Borda along with Eugene Scossa, a prominent farmer in the county and John Besio, a man in his employee, who were arrested for operating a still. A search of the Scossa barn revealed a stash of more than 500 gallons of moonshine and an equal amount of mash, together with a complete still. It had been common knowledge that a still was operating on the Scossa ranch for more than a year and yet no one was willing to divulge the source of so much pleasure. January 31, 1926 saw an end of the 20 year existence of what was once Meyers Mercantile and then Farmer's Mercantile Company in Minden when fire destroyed the entire building.

Left: Minden Rotary and Carson Valley Kiwanis club members at Minden Inn for Kiwanis charter dinner, circa 1927. *(DCHS 289.G.2)*

Right: J.B.D., Susie Dick and G.M.W. pose in front of their car in 1920. *(DCHS 137-H237a)*

Above: Minden-Bridgeport Stage (car) in front of Ritchford Hotel on Main Street in Gardnerville, 1920s. *(DCHS 2007.003.085)*

Right: Howard Bros. store in the Odd Fellows building, circa 1920. The store was established April 29, 1910 by E.C. Howard and Frank R. Howard. From left are Frank R. Howard, Ernest C. Howard, Loyd Darby, Josephine Raycraft and Ester Menzel. *(DCHS 1029.G.003b)*

Far right: Susie Dick, Washoe. *(DCHS 0136.G.0009)*

Above: Basketball team at Douglas County High School standing on the front stairs of the school in 1923. *(DCHS 2006.042.004)*

Right: Flour mill of the Douglas Milling and Power Company, Gardnerville. Twelve-horse team and wagons loading sacks of flour. Henry Hellwinkel, teamster and Fred Sarman on loading dock. *(DCHS 0136-G-58)*

Above: Block D Society Club at Douglas County High School in 1923. *(DCHS 2006.042.001)*

Left: View of Minden Flour Milling Co., and Meyers Mercantile with early automobiles, circa 1920. *(DCHS 0263-H-168)*

Above: Artesian wells in operation at the Dangberg Ranch, circa 1921. *(DCHS 5-G-125)*

Right: Horse-drawn sleigh in front of Minden Grocery in the 1920s. *(DCHS 2007.009.016)*

Top: Wagons loaded with hay, to be stacked, for winter livestock feed. *(DCHS 0005-G-289)*

Left: Gardnerville Fourth of July Parade in 1922. *(DCHS 0005.6.191)*

Above: View of downtown in Minden Dry Goods Company, C.O.D. Garage, and Minden Inn, circa 1925. *(DCHS 2007.009.030)*

Right: Central School class of 1923. *(DCHS 267.G.0004)*

The 1930s

The Great Depression came home to Douglas County as Valley farmers watched the price of butter and meat drop. Then in September 1931, bank examiners took over the Douglas County Farmer's Bank in Gardnerville, which had more than 100 depositors.

Bank collapses weren't limited to Douglas County. In 1932, the state declared a 12-day bank holiday after the Wingfield banks collapsed.

Holding the line were the officers of the Farmer's Bank of Carson Valley in Minden. After the banks was allowed to close, bank president William Dressler and cashier William Wennhold went to San Francisco to secure enough cash to reopen after only three days.

In recognition of the hard times, tax rates were cut and county officials accepted pay cuts.

The 1930s also saw the legalization of gambling in Nevada. The day county commissioners signed off on the new law, a proposal for a casino along the state line at Lake Tahoe was reported.

The year 1932 was the last time Douglas County voted for a Democrat for president, Franklin Delano Roosevelt.

According to the U.S. Census, there were 1,840 people living in Douglas County in 1930.

The decade saw both the towns of Gardnerville and Minden paving their streets.

Left: "Two teams aligned," of horses and scrapers clearing the fields for planting in the Minden area, 1934. *(DCHS 0005-G-265)*

Right: Business block of Genoa, circa 1932. *(DCHS 0120-G-054a)*

Right: Douglas County Court House, circa 1930. *(DCHS 2004.031.055)*

Below: 4-H Club camp on the old universtiy farm and apple orchard, circa 1931. From left, Harlan Fricke, Marvin Settelmeyer, Delbert Allerman, Walter Heidtman, Ged Gansberg, Albert Heidtman, Hoover Hansen, Bill Campbell, Gus Campbell, William White, Arvin Jacobsen, William Stodieck, Lester Stodieck, Emory Graunke, Duane Allerman, Jack White, Lawrence Jacobsen, Herbert Jacobsen, John Reiman, Curtis Gansberg, Budd Dressler. *(DCHS 2004.031.006a-b)*

Above: Post Office, Minden Mercantile and the CVIC Hall in Minden, 1930s.
(DCHS 2006.083.009)

Right: Interior of Ellis's Minden Grocery, circa 1930. *(DCHS 2007.009.028)*

Above: Cattle grazing on the Dangberg Ranch, 1934. *(DCHS 0005-G-261A)*

Below: Luke and Fritz Neddenriep along with Zelda Heitman go for a buggy ride at the Heitman Ranch, circa 1930. *(DCHS 0050.G.002)*

Above: Adams residence in Genoa, 1932. *(DCHS 0120.6.005)*

Below: Dangberg Ranch animals, Minden, March 1934. *(DCHS 0005-G-2588)*

Left: A horse-drawn tank wagon in the Carson Valley Day Parade in the late 1930s. *(DCHS 2007.009.010)*

Bottom left: Minden grade school football team and students in the 1930s at the bandstand in Minden Park. Standing on bandstand from left, unknown, Delphina Biaggi, unknown, unknown, unknown, Howard Godecke, Paula Springmeyer, unknown, Wilma Smith, Billie Jean Stinsen, Yvonne Chango, Jessie McInnis, Kathryn Krummes, Verona Thomas, unknown, Ida Biaggi, Phyllis Dangberg, Majorie Johnson, Luetta Dressler, and Harriet Morrison. Seated on bandstand, Marion Anderson, Muriel Biaggi, Marie Grenada, and Fritzi Jane Neddenriep. Standing in front of bandstand, Bill Andrews, Delbert Allerman, Marvin Settelmeyer, and Sammy Joe. Kneeling, Bruce Roberts, Tommy Chambers, Budd Dressler, Elwood Johnson, unknown, Guy Anderson, and John Uhart. *(DCHS 0238.G.006b)*

Below: Two men in the Carson Valley Day Parade featuring the unique "Gray Ghost," circa 1935. *(DCHS 2007.009.009)*

75

Left: Douglas County High School Football Team, 1934-35. *(DCHS 1008.G.2a)*

Opposite: Douglas County High School Band, 1934. *(DCHS 0022.G.0001m)*

Below: Douglas County High School student body in Gardnerville, 1934. *(DCHS 159.G.2)*

Right: Minden School students, September 21, 1938. *(DCHS 0260-G-0099E)*

Bottom right: Douglas County High School, circa 1935. The school now houses the Carson Valley Museum and Cultural Center. *(DCHS 0334.G.1b)*

Below: Douglas County High School students enjoy the day outside of the front entrance, circa 1935. *(DCHS 0334.G.1a)*

Above: The majestic Reynolds Peak in August of 1937. *(DCHS 0137.H.233a)*

Right: The Nevada Club, circa 1936. The club had expanded and improved since it opened five years earlier. *Courtesy Lake Tahoe Historical Society*

Far right: Carson Valley Day Parade in 1938 with the first rider as Ged Gansberg and the second rider as Ruth Lunderg. *(DCHS 0275.G.012)*

Below: Cattle drive passing Harrah's Stateline Casino, circa 1959. *Courtesy Lake Tahoe Historical Society*

The 1940s

World War II was the most significant event of the 1940s, and Carson Valley went above and beyond to ensure America's victory.

Drafting of Douglas County men into the U.S. Military began in 1940 and continued throughout the war, with hundreds of Douglas County residents risking everything for their country, including at least 16 Native Americans from the Dresslerville Washoe Tribe.

After Pearl Harbor in 1941, Douglas County began staging trial "blackouts" to prepare for enemy bombers infiltrating the west coast. Everyday citizens became crucial to the war effort. Valley farmers helped with metal, rubber and gasoline rationing. Local businesses, churches, schools and other institutions participated in seven different war loan drives. Douglas County repeatedly exceeded its quota for sale revenue of war bonds and stamps, helping fund the war in Europe and the South Pacific.

In 1942, future Sen. Lawrence Jacobsen from Gardnerville, then 22 years-old, spoke at the Minden Inn recounting his experience aboard a ship at the Battle of Coral Sea where he used a deck gun to shoot three enemy planes out of the air.

Carson Valley suffered the losses of some of its most prominent pioneers: Marie Settelmeyer, Patrick J. Hickey, Margaret Dangberg and H.F. Dangberg Jr. who founded the town of Minden.

Much of the 1940s was an effort to preserve an era past while encouraging modern improvements. Senator Will F. Dressler and Assemblyman George Hussman lobbied hard to preserve and reconstruct Mormon Station.

Left: Gasoline engine powered threshing machine, circa 1940. *(DCHS 0136-G-024)*

Right: Jean Wurst in front of Minden home, 1940s. *(DCHS 0330.G.0002i)*

Above: Street scene in Gardnerville, 1940s. *(DCHS 2007.003.045)*

Left: Interior of the Overland Hotel, circa 1940. *(DCHS 2006.058.127)*

Right: Jean and Jack Wurst at a circus at Camp Minden. *(DCHS 0330.G.0002c)*

Bottom right: A man riding his bike smoking his pipe through town during Carson Valley Days, circa 1940. *(DCHS 1033.G.003e)*

Below: Street scene after a heavy snow storm, 1940s. *(DCHS 0026.G.002)*

Right: Downtown Minden during the filming of "Chicken Every Sunday" with a horse-drawn wagon and people in costume, circa 1940. *(DCHS 2003.054.026)*

Below: Downtown Minden during the filming of "Chicken Every Sunday" in 1940. *(DCHS 2006.027.091)*

Above: Street Scene, Bridgeport, Calif., 1940s. *(DCHS 1037.6..001)*

Left: Kingsberry Grade (old road), circa 1940. *(DCHS 334-G-lj)*

Below: The early 1940s Minden, Nevada Rotary Club on the steps of the Minden Inn. Back row from left: Farmer, Richard Bassman (wife was niece of Dorretta Heise), County Clerk, Hans Jepsen, Owner of Minden Mercantile, John Ellis, Station Master of Virginia & Truckee Railway, Walter Fisher, Sheriff of Douglas County, Wm. Park. Middle row from left: Mgr. of Union Oil Co, C. W. "Slim" Roberts, Bookkeeper of Dangberg Land & Livestock, Lyle McInnis, District Attorney, Grover Krick, Cashier at Farmer's Bank of Carson Valley, Wm. H. Wennhold, Owner of Block's Cleaners, John Block, Hardware Store owner, Wm. Nelson. Front row: Owner of Dangberg Land & Livestock, H.F. Dangberg, Plumbing, George P. Dangberg (cousin to John & F. H. Dangberg), Owner of Dangberg Land & Livestock, John Dangberg, Owner of Minden Inn, Frank Andrews. *(DCHS 0142.G.003)*

Right: Engine No. 27 coming through Carson Valley, 1942. *(DCHS 137-H-142)*

Far right: Virginia & Truckee Engine's No. 11 and 27 at Minden, September 1941. *(DCHS 263-G-5)*

Below: Fettic's Exchange, Genoa. *(DCHS 0136.G.207)*

Right: Minden Grammar School, 1942. First row, Wayne Bassman, Henry Tietje, Bobby Thomsen, Harlan Anderson, Harold Anderson, Arthur McMasters, Ronald Wilcks, Edwin Hasse, and Roy Thomsen. Second row, Nancy Sharp, Carl Johnson, Harold Coon, Tommy Mack, Patricia Cordes, Esther Tietdje, Viola Tietdje, Marcia Robinson, Mazie Smith, Margaret Stodieck, and Marcelle Hansen. Third row, Teacher Alyze Savage, Bob Summers, Donna Sexsmith, Mildred Cordes, Marlena Neddenriep, Irene Haase, Larry McMasters, Hilda Leehman, Carl Carstensen, Jim Summers, Andy Aldax, John Jepsen, Ruby Schacht, and unknown. Fourth row, Gerald Zenola, Richard Barham, Carroll Cahoon, unknown, unknown, Barbara Sexsmith, Lorraine Bassman, Carol Judd, unknown, and Bob Jepsen. Fifth row, R. Baumgartner, Roland Dreyer, Harriet Hellwinkel, Loretta Bassman, Lois Lange, Alta Tietje, Lois Schacht, Beverly Blondin, Carolyn Godecke, Thelma Winkelman, Barbara Bussey, Forrest Tietje, and Steven Achard. Sixth row, John Summers,, Leslie Thran, unknown, Joyce Gilbert, Nancy Barsty, Patricia Lange, Betty Thomsen, Louanna Tietje, Elinor Godecke, Lois Cordes, Henry (Bud) Berrum Jr., and Billy Johnson. Seventh row, John Lundergreen, Bob Heitman, Donald Judd, Bill Wennhold, Mildred Dreyer, Shirley Lundergreen, Ray Jepsen, and Nevada Wise. Eighth row, Music Teacher Lois Brooks, Principal Harold Curran, Teacher Bertha Cardinal, and Stella Manfrina. *(DCHS 2004.036.010)*

Bottom right: Lois Brooks, a teacher at Minden Grammar School from 1936-1942. *(DCHS 2005.006.010)*

Below: Gardnerville Elementary School, 1943. *(DCHS 2005.003.001)*

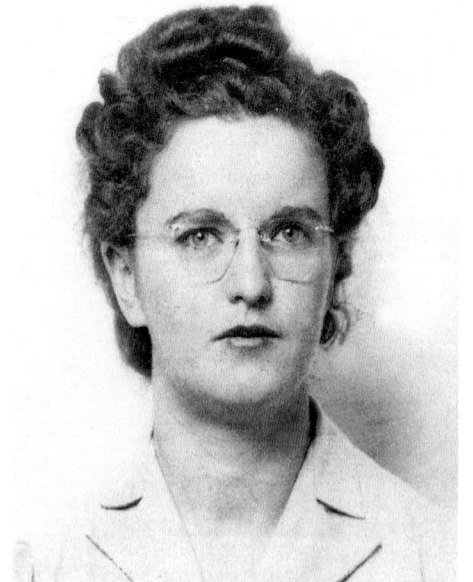

Above: Douglas County High School faculty, circa 1940. *(DCHS 2002.018.010)*

Right: Minden School, 1943. *(DCHS 2004.036.011)*

Bottom right: Douglas County High School Basketball Team, 1943. Photo includes, from back left, Tom Isozaki, Bob Mullens, Fred Shawe, Jimmy Miller, Orvel Canonic, Coach Wittmore, Jerry Busick, Mark Bray, Gordon Fricke, Bill Godecke, Fred Minchin. *(DCHS 0351.G.6c)*

Below: Douglas County Band. *(DCHS 0022.G0001a)*

Above: Loading bales of hay onto the back of a truck. *(DCHS 0005-G-153)*

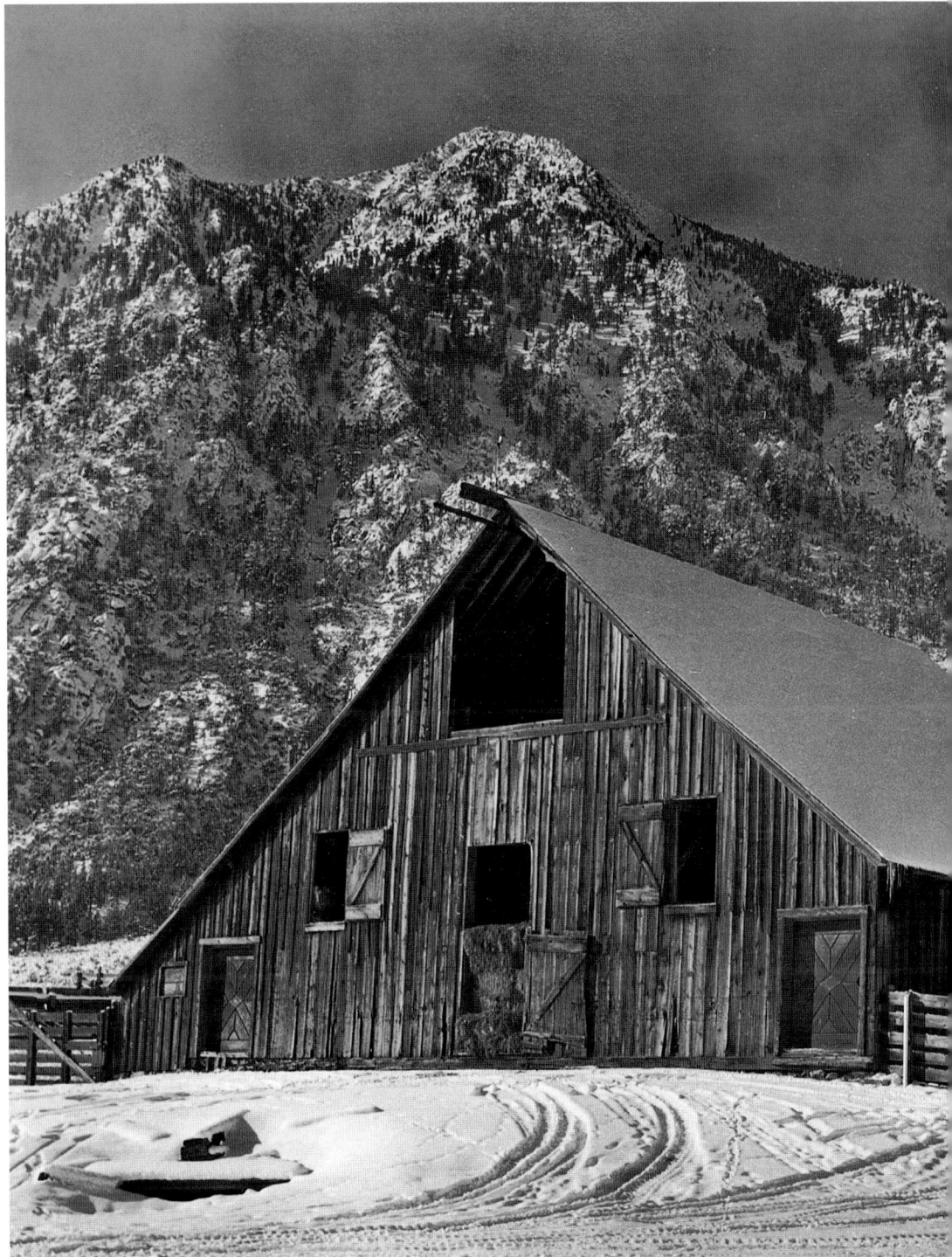

Right: Scossa Ranch barn. *(DCHS 136-G-22)*

Above: Extension agents, Ray Cox and Otto Schulz, and pickers check the crop before the heavy equipment moves in, 1945. *(DCHS 0205-G-002g)*

Right: Heavy equipment used for potato farming in Carson Valley, 1940s. *(DCHS 0205-G-002)*

Opposite: Potato harvesting crew in Carson Valley, 1940s. *(DCHS 0205-G-002g)*

Left: Ski jumper at the Snowshoe Thompson Memorial Cross Country Ski Race in 1946. *(DCHS 0131.G.430c)*

Bottom left: Winner of the Snowshoe Thompson Memorial Cross Country Ski Race award for the Douglas Country Ski Club in 1946. *(DCHS 0131.G.430a)*

Opposite: Aerial view of the Carson Valley with the Sierra Nevadas and Lake Tahoe in the back, circa 1945. *(DCHS 0137.H.356)*

Below: Oliver's Club, just east of the state line opened in the 1930s. By the 1940s, when this photo was taken, it was Tahoe Village complete with neon signs.
Courtesy Lake Tahoe Historical Society

Above: Minden Rotary Club members, 1948. In the photo are Archie and Daphne Safely, Ken and Marie Blondin, Roy and Ina Crowell, Wilbur and Velma Stodieck, Lou and Vi Frakes and Loyd and Vernita Springmeyer. *(DCHS 2006-094-001)*

Right: Minden Grammar School basketball team, 1947. Front row are Arlen (Pudge) Turria, Phil Scoggins, Gary Lundergreen John Jepsen and Bobby Sarasola. Back row are Ortey Neller, Louis Micheo, Bob Jepsen, Jim Summers and Ron Wilcks. Archie Safley was the principal and coach. *(DCHS 2006-035-001)*

Below: Minden School students, 1945. Front row are Robert Sarasola, Henry Tietje, Arlen Turria, Julian Larrouy and Harold Anderson. Middle row are Andy Aldax, Roy Corstensen, Jim Summers, _____Beach, Sandra Byers, Marlena Neddenriep, Wanda Clark and Larry McMasters. Back row are, Robert Jepsen, John Jepsen, unidentified, Miss Gillies, Anita Oelschlaeger, Anita Prudenciado, Phyllis Wilslef and Harlan Anderson. *(DCHS 0260-G-0099J)*

Above: Douglas County High School band, circa 1949. *(DCHS 0351.G.VI.b)*

Below: Douglas County High School Cheerleading Squad, circa 1949. *(DCHS 1049.G.1a)*

The 1950s

The 1950s opened with the end of an era when the last regularly scheduled Virginia & Truckee Railway engine steamed into Minden. The V&T served the Carson Valley since the new town of Minden was founded by H.F. Dangberg Jr. in 1906. However, along with the fresh food hauled out of Carson Valley, the railroad carried a heavy debt. After bouts with receivership and losing $102,421, the railroad that once carried its weight in gold made its last trip in June 1950.

But just as that door was closing, a hatch was opening in the form of regularly scheduled airline flights courtesy of Bonanza Air. The orange-nosed aircraft were a daily sight at the airport serving both Minden and Carson City for several years.

It wasn't long before the airline followed the Valley's rail connection into history when they suspended service in the mid-1950s again reducing the number of ways residents were connected with the outside world.

The summer of 1951 saw the celebration of Genoa's centennial as Nevada's first permanent settlement.

Sports were an important part of Valley life and it was front page news when Douglas High School won its first football title by taking the Western Conference after an undefeated season and the championship basketball team featured ace shooter Johnny Borda, who racked up 403 points in 18 games for a school record.

It was the 1950s that Carson Valley lost its chronicler for the prior four decades, Bert Selkirk, who died Feb. 19, 1954. Valley agricultural empire founder H.F. Dangberg's last son, John, died in 1958.

Left: The Harbor at Bijou Park, circa 1950. *(DCHS 2006-048-006)*

Right: Last run of the V&T train into Minden, 1950. Men standing on the tracks are Emery W. Graunke, Don Hellwinkel, Dan Hellwinkel, Lou Coles and Scotchy Mack. Stan Peyton is playing taps on a bugle. *(DCHS 137-H-143)*

Right: Twin States Casino, Stateline, circa 1950. *(DCHS 0334.G.002x)*

Opposite: Group posing for the photo in front of the club at Stateline, winter of 1951. *(DCHS 0334.G.002W)*

Below: The Nevada Stateline. *Courtesy Douglas County Historical Society*

Left: John Jepsen of the 1950-51 Douglas County High School Basketball Team. *(DCHS 0401.G.0001)*

Far left: Danny Kurtz of the 1950 Douglas County High School Football Team. *(DCHS 0401.G.0001)*

Bottom left: Sideline during a 1950 Douglas County High School football game. *(DCHS 0401.G.0001)*

Opposite: Louie Micheo, Martin Johnson, and Don Hansen posing a game of horseshoes for the 1950-51 Douglas County High school yearbook. *(DCHS 0401.G.0001)*

Below: John Borda makes a quick cut on the basketball court for the Douglas High School team of 1950-51. *(DCHS 0401.G.0001)*

Right: The Genoa Centennial Celebration in 1951 with Governor Charles Russell making a presentation. *(DCHS 0131.G.0633a)*

Below: The Genoa Centennial Celebration in 1951. *(DCHS 0131.G.0633)*

Right: Nevada Governor Charles Russell, right, with Hans Meyer-Kassel, center, artist of the oil painting on the wall, at the 100th anniversary celebration of the Mormon Station on July 14, 1951. *(DCHS 0120.G.001)*

Bottom right: Swearing in ceremony of Douglas County public officials in Minden, 1951. From left, district attorney, Grover Krick, E. Fork, district constable, Oscar Lundergreen, justice of the peace, Bert Selkirk, recorder-auditor, Ethel Schacht, county assessor, Harry Winkelman, Lake Tahoe constable, Mr. Stambaugh, clerk and treasurer, Hans Jepsen. *(DCHS 2002.45.001)*

Below: Bert Selkirk, owner and publisher of the Record-Courier, 1951. He started as an employee of the newspaper and then owner from 1908-1944. He spent 52 years in the newspaper business. *(DCHS 0136-G-058)*

Right: Players Irene Marshall, Pat Cordes (with glass protection) & Roberta Cochran from the 1953 Douglas County High School Women's Basketball Team. *(DCHS 2006.035.003)*

Opposite: Last few minutes of the 1953 Zone Championship game Douglas County High School played with Reno High. Coach took the boys out after it was positive that Douglas had won and put the second team in. The players are, from left, Martin Johnson, Louie Micheo, Stan Summers, Gary Lundergreen, and Jim Callahan. *(DCHS 2006.035.002)*

Below: Fans cheering for the 1953 Douglas County High School Basketball Team at the Zone Tournament at the University of Nevada gym in Reno. *(DCHS 2006.035.004)*

Right: The East Fork Hotel float in the Carson Valley Day Parade. The merry-go-round is pulled by a jeep. Riding the merry-go-round from left to right, Joyce Borda, Angie Borda, Gina Borda, and Darlene Oxoby with Eddie, Paul, and Dana Borda in the Jeep and Worth Borda as the driver in 1953. *(DCHS 2007.010.001)*

Bottom right: Frances Settelmeyer and Santa in Gardnerville, circa 1954.
Courtesy Douglas County Historical Society

Left: Frank Yparraguirre, owner of Perry's Dry Goods Store. *(DCHS 2006.058.014)*

Below: C. C. Crosley, Nevada magazine publisher, circa 1955. *(DCHS 0334.G.002r)*

Left: Diane Springmeyer, Callahan and Linda Shaw Reid at Carson Valley Days, circa 1955. *(DCHS 2003.054.007)*

Bottom left: Carson Valley Day Parade crossing in front of the Minden Mercantile Company, circa 1955. *(DCHS 2006.028.002)*

Opposite: Herefords on the Rocky Creek Ranch. *(DCHS 0136-G-16)*

Below: Children in front of the "Search the Scriptures" float for the Carson Valley Day Parade, circa 1955. *(DCHS 2006.028.003)*

Right: View of Jobs Peak from the old site of Sheridan, 1950s. *(DCHS 136-G-15)*

Opposite: Clouds rolling in on the beautiful Sierra Nevada Mountains behind Carson Valley, circa 1955. *(DCHS 0137.H.230)*

Below: North of Genoa looking south on Foothill Road, circa 1955. *(DCHS 0136.G.11)*

Right: Gardnerville Elementary School. Mary Mack's second grade class in 1957. *Courtesy Douglas County Historical Society*

Far right: Gardnerville School in 1959. *(DCHS 0281.G.0025m)*

Below: Gardnerville School in 1956, taught by Mrs. Roberts. *(DCHS 0281.G.0025a)*

Left: View looking south to Jobs Peak from Kiwanis Point, 1950s. *(DCHS 136-G-12)*

The 1960s & '70s

Between the turn of the century and 1960, Douglas County's population grew from 1,535 people to 3,481, according to the U.S. Census. In the two decades between 1960 and 1980 it grew nearly six times to 19,921.

Most of that growth came during the 1970s when people attracted to the county's natural and agricultural beauty moved here. Stateline grew upward, from a collection of small casinos to the high rises there today. Population growth at Lake Tahoe led to the construction of all three Lake Tahoe schools during the two decades.

The Gardnerville Ranchos was born in 1965 and would grow to be Douglas County's single largest community. Douglas County High School in Gardnerville became Douglas High School in Minden, when the new school was built in 1975.

Closing out the decade, the agricultural empire built by the Dangberg family over more than a century passed out of its hands when it was sold to a California consortium in 1978. The ranch would never be the same size again, but the small piece where H.F. Dangberg founded his empire has been preserved as a state park.

The 1970s closed when an extortionist detonated a bomb in Harvey's Casino.

Left: Cheerleading Squad of Douglas County High School, 1962. Photo includes Debbie Haase Byers, Sherri Simmons Fry, Ginny Van, Eileen Jones Decker. The uniforms were made by Alice Haase. *(DCHS 1023.G.1b)*

Right: Brick Hellwinkel, owner of the C.O.D. is handing the keys of the driver's education vehicle over to the superintendent of Douglas County schools Gene Scarcelli. To the left is Walt Powers, the driver's education instructor and to the right of Gene Scarcelli is Principal Jerome Etchegoyhen and Don Hellwinkel (Brick's son). Photo, 1964. *(DCHS 0201.G.31)*

Left: Washo, from left, Gary Frank, Clara Frank and Eleanor Snookey, dressed in attire for the 1961 Centennial at Genoa. *(DCHS 0136.G.0008)*

Above: Gordon and JoAnne Fricke on their wedding day in the 1960s. *Courtesy Douglas County Historical Society*

Right: Raymond Griswold in front of the Sanford home on Esmeralda Ave. in Minden on Valentine's Day, 1960. *(DCHS 2003.054.009)*

Above: Christmas Dinner at the Pasek home in Minden, circa 1962. Well-known local photographer Juanita Schubert, far right, joined the family, from left, Gerry, John, Mrs. Lavern Pasek and Gene. The photo was taken by Dr. John Pasek.
Courtesy Douglas County Historical Society

Left: Trinity Lutheran Church Vacation Bible School students, circa 1963. *(DCHS 2006.053.003)*

Top left: Minden Primary School, first grade students, 1963. Included in the photo are Roger Bachseini, Mark Kizer, Paul Logan, Bryan Lewallen, Keran Moore, Sheree Johnson, Renee Presto, Peggy Willard, Marsha Smith, Phil Nalder, Aron Smokey, Rick Bartells, L.S. Robinson, Debbie Hellwinkel, Patty Melnick, Valarie Morrison and Terri Witherspoon. *(DCHS 0281-G-0025p)*

Top right: Nevada State Cow Belles Lourinda Wines, Marie Stewart, and Anna Dressler. *(DCHS 0210.G.008)*

Right: Confirmation Class in Gardnerville. Included in picture are Bill Jepsen, Charlotte Settelmeyer, Roger Stodieck, Pastor Leising, Judi Thran, Bob Gansberg, Dan Henningsen, and Mark Hussman, circa 1964.
Courtesy Douglas County Historical Society

Above: Carson Valley Day Celebrations. Lawrence Settelmeyer pictured on left with Bill Lampe in Gardnerville, 1965.
Courtesy Douglas County Historical Society

Left: Douglas County Fire Department. *(DCHS 2007-009-005)*

Right: Branding cattle on the Scossa Ranch, Carson Valley. *(DCHS 0136-G-17)*

Above: Separating cows and two month old calves prior to marketing and branding, Dressler Ranch. *(DCHS 0137-H-100)*

Right: The Nevada Club in the 1960s. *Courtesy Lake Tahoe Historical Society*

Above: The Stateline Country Club was one of the first gambling clubs at Lake Tahoe in 1931. By the 1960s it had expanded and was also offering fine dining. *Courtesy Lake Tahoe Historical Society*

Left: Surrey in front of the Glenbrook Inn. *Courtesy Douglas County Historical Society*

Right: Harold "Friday" Park sitting behind the wheel of a Douglas County fire truck in April of 1970. *(DCHS 2007.009.004)*

Above: Albert Settelmeyer (back) and "Pete" milk the cows in the newly created bacteria-free environment. *(DCHS 0137-H-136)*

Left: Unidentified little girl on horseback, 1969. *Courtesy Douglas County Historical Society*

Right: Sally Lyda, Record-Courier staff, 1970s. *(DCHS 2003-002-002)*

Far right: Sally Lyda and Joyce Hollister, employees of The Record-Courier, 1978. *(DCHS 2006-58-417)*

Above: Candy Dance Kids at the commissioners meeting. From left, Judy Brierly with her children, Commissioner Dan Hickey, and Commissioner Ken Kjer in 1977. *(DCHS 2006.058.314)*

Left: The opening of the senior center in 1977. From left, Commissioner Dan Hickey, Soroptimist Laurie Hickey, Soroptomist and Librarian Yvonne Saddler, Gary Stone, Director George Everman, and Rev. Emil Leising. *(DCHS 2006.058.234)*

Above: Douglas County Recorder-Auditor, Ethel Schacht, in front, and her staff, 1971. From left, Joanne Bruns, Starla Fettic-Smith, Jean Grimm, Jackie O'Leary. *(DCHS 2002.45.002)*

Above: The Douglas High School homecoming marching band in the Carson Valley Day Parade in 1979. *(DCHS 2006.058.179)*

Left: Mrs. Catherine T. McGurrin, Colonel Reese's Granddaughter, and Mr. Beattie, Hampton S. Beattie's son, at the potluck picnic of Carson Valley Historical Society in July, 1977. *(DCHS 0120.G.042)*

Right: The dedication of the new wing of Young at Heart in 1979. Holding the shovel is Pastor Emil Leising and Yvonne Saddler. *(DCHS 2006.058.132)*

Above: Discussing the Harvey's bombing, Tahoe-Douglas Fire Chief Bruce Kanoff and Sheriff Jerry Maple. *(DCHS 2006.058.407)*

Left: The ground-breaking of the warehouse in 1979. From left, Commissioner Dan Hickey, Norm Bullinger, Commissioner Gary Stone, Commissioner Gene Osborne, Derrell Moore, Bob Skibinski, and Tony Loring. *(DCHS 2006.058.278)*

Right: The damage to the Harveys Casino and Resort after the bombing. *(DCHS 2006.058.083)*

Right: The police blockade set up during the initial investigation of the Harveys bombing. *(DCHS 2006.058.082)*

Above: The damage done to Harveys Casino and Resort immediately following the bombing. *(DCHS 2006.058.406)*

Left: At a press conference, the actual photograph of the bomb used during Harveys bombing is revealed. *(DCHS 2006.058.408)*